dyes & decoration

HAZEL KING

Heinemann
LIBRARY

www.heinemann.co.uk
Visit our website to find out more information about Heinemann Library books.

To order:
 Phone 44 (0) 1865 888066
 Send a fax to 44 (0) 1865 314091
 Visit the Heinemann Bookshop at www.heinemann.co.uk to browse our catalogue and order online.

First published in Great Britain by Heinemann Library,
Halley Court, Jordan Hill, Oxford OX2 8EJ,
a division of Reed Educational and Professional Publishing Ltd.
Heinemann is a registered trademark of Reed Educational & Professional Publishing Limited.

OXFORD MELBOURNE AUCKLAND
JOHANNESBURG BLANTYRE GABORONE
IBADAN PORTSMOUTH NH (USA) CHICAGO

© Reed Educational and Professional Publishing Ltd 2000
The moral right of the proprietor has been asserted.

Designed by AMR
Illustrations by Art Construction
Originated by Ambassador Litho Ltd
Printed in Hong Kong/China

ISBN 0 431 10562 6

04 03 02 01 00
10 9 8 7 6 5 4 3 2 1

British Library Cataloguing in Publication Data
King, Hazel
 Dyes & decoration. – (Trends in textile technology)
 1.Dyes and dyeing – Juvenile literature 2.Color in the
 textile industry – Juvenile literature
 I.Title
 667.3

Acknowledgements
The Publishers would like to thank the following for permission to reproduce photographs:
Bridgeman Art Library/Burghley House Collection: p36 Corbis p9, p22; Eye Ubiquitous: p18, Paul Seheult p27; Heinemann: G Boden pp11, 13, 15, 17, 25, 29, 30, 31, 33, 34, 38, 40; Novara Group p10; Trip: M Ewing p4, Chris Parker p37, Streano/Havens, H Rogers, Eric Pelham p43

Cover photograph reproduced with permission of Corbis.

Our thanks to Andy Rumsby for his comments in the preparation of this book.

Every effort has been made to contact copyright holders of any material reproduced in this book. Any omissions will be rectified in subsequent printings if notice is given to the Publisher.

Any words appearing in the text in bold, **like this**, are explained in the glossary.

J1/4, 523
£10·99

contents

colour, wonderful colour

Colour can inspire. Colour can influence. Colour can have a huge impact on all our lives. Consider for a moment some aspects of life that are affected by colour – traffic lights, uniforms, football strips, skin colour, food, flags, make-up, funerals, weddings... the list goes on.

Searching for something new to wear gives a good insight into the importance of colour in textiles. If you are browsing through shops it is likely that you will first pick up an item of clothing because you are attracted to the colour, before you consider its style or size. Of course, the effect of colour is not limited to clothing. You can give a room a cosy feel or a chilly effect just by changing the colour scheme. Brochures used for choosing paint illustrate this really well, as they often show examples of rooms decorated using various shades of colour (also known as hues).

Colour choice

Colour can sometimes help in creating a particular effect. The look of an interior design is affected by the furniture, by how it is positioned, and by the furnishings and fabrics as well as by other items in the room. In addition to colour, clothes can provide a particular effect by the choice and cut of fabric, any accessories or **embellishments** and, of course, the person wearing the outfit.

Colours change according to fashion, and fashion reflects the values of the society for any given period of time. Today our society is concerned with environmental issues and this is quite evident in some of our fashions. Many people want natural colours to go with their preference for natural fibres and fabrics. In contrast, the celebrations for the millennium seem set to continue for some time in fashion terms, as clothes become bold and bright, with lots of orange and plenty of clashing colour.

Seeing the light

Light plays a crucial role in our ability to see colours. It sounds obvious to say we can see colour only when light is available, but the light from the sun actually contains all colours – so, where there is no light, there is no colour. As sunlight passes through raindrops, a rainbow is formed because the light is

As sunlight passes through raindrops, a rainbow is formed. The main colours of the rainbow are red, orange, yellow, green, blue, indigo and violet.

split up, enabling us to see the main colours of the spectrum. The spectrum is visible light divided into all the colours. The colours are red, orange, yellow, green, blue, indigo and violet.

Absorbing colours

When light falls on an object certain colours of the spectrum are absorbed and others are reflected. The colours we see are those that are reflected by the object. For example, if someone enters the room wearing a blue wig, we know it is blue because the wig is absorbing all the light (containing all colours of the spectrum) except blue, which is reflected back for us to see. If, however, the wig had been white then all the colours of the spectrum would have been reflected. Black, on the other hand, is seen as black because it absorbs all the colours in the spectrum of light, and none is reflected back.

Colour characteristics

All colours have two main characteristics. They have a value, which is a measure of their lightness or darkness, and they have an intensity, which indicates the strength of the colour. By adding white to a colour you create a TINT, and by adding black you produce a SHADE.

A wheel of colour

The colour wheel is a way of representing colours. The colours are divided into three types: primary, secondary and tertiary.
- PRIMARY colours are red, yellow and blue.

▼ The colours are divided into three types: primary, secondary and tertiary.

- SECONDARY colours are orange, green and violet, and are made by mixing two primary colours together. For example, mix red and yellow and create orange.
- TERTIARY colours are a mix of primary and secondary colours. So, red (primary) may be mixed with orange (secondary), and so on.

Colour schemes

A whole array of colour schemes are available. A monochromatic scheme is based on just one colour, so it uses variations of that colour in different intensities. An analogous scheme contains three or more colours close together on the colour wheel so they harmonize with one another. A complementary scheme uses colours from opposite sides of the colour wheel. A triad scheme is made from three colours of equal distance from each other on the colour wheel.

changing colours

We take it for granted that our textile items come in such a wonderful array of colours. But this is possible only when a dye is added. A dye is a substance added to textiles in order to give them colour. Originally people dyed yarns and fabrics with natural dyes such as plant leaves and berries. Then, during the 1850s, a scientist called William H Perkins discovered **synthetic** dyes, and a whole new world of bright and bold colours was unleashed.

Colourfastness

Dyes work by absorbing some of the light and reflecting back the colour that is seen. They have to be applied to the fibre, yarn or fabric, and usually this is done with water, either cold or hot. However, dyes would not be much use unless they could be made to be fast, or **colourfast**, which means they will not wash out or rub off. Sometimes colours do fade over time, but this effect may be desired, for example, with denim jeans.

Mordants

In order to make a dye fast, a **mordant** is added during the dyeing process. A mordant is a chemical that can 'fix' the dye so it will not wash out or fade. The various types of **dyestuffs** require different types of mordant, but the most usual ones are alum, tin, chrome and iron. Some mordants can be toxic, so people working with them must take great care.

Natural dyes

Like weaving and spinning, natural dyeing is a very old craft. Natural dyes produce 'countryside' shades – muted colours that tone easily with one another. Natural dyeing has a very 'green' image. Not only does it produce natural hues (colours), it can also involve recycling by using onion skins or carrot tops to dye fabric, instead of throwing them away!

The first colours used for dyeing were acquired from animal and vegetable sources. Sepia brown was obtained from cuttlefish, while mosses and lichen provided green colours. The South American beetle is a source for cochineal pink, and flowers such as saffron and marigold supply yellows and golds. Bark called logwood bark can produce shades of brown and black. Some natural dyestuffs and the colours they produce are shown below.

Blues/purples/mauves
Blackberries Elderberries Marjoram flower buds Sloe berries Blueberries
Reds/pinks
Madder roots Sorrel roots Red cabbage leaves
Greens
Apple bark Bracken Privet leaves Tomato leaves and stems

Indigo blue

During Roman times the woad plant (*Isatis tinctoria*) was used to produce the colour indigo, a shade of blue. It was once the most important crop in central Europe but today it is making a comeback in England!

The Ministry of Agriculture and some companies are running a research project into the development of a new crop of woad to produce natural indigo. Traditionally the extraction process for woad took twelve weeks, but now the time taken from harvesting the crop to producing a blue dye takes just twelve minutes.

Natural indigo is usually used to dye denim. India and China supply most of this natural dye to Britain.

Yellows/golds
Marigold
Onion skins
Stinging nettles
Lily-of-the-valley leaves

Fawns/beiges
Dock leaves
Heather
Lichen
Pine cones, crushed

Browns
Walnut shells, crushed and soaked
Elder leaves
Dock leaves

Dyeing time

Try some natural dyeing for yourself.

Resources
- a cooker hob
- a pair of rubber gloves
- an apron
- an old sieve or colander
- an old large saucepan
- about 250g of natural dyestuff (see the charts below)
- an old plastic container (e.g. ice cream tub)
- 250ml acetic acid (vinegar)
- about 100g wool fleece
- a little washing-up liquid

Method
1 Wearing an apron and rubber gloves, put the dyestuff in the old saucepan with 500ml of water. Bring to the boil and simmer for about 30 minutes or until the water has turned a strong colour.
2 To remove the dyestuff, strain the water into the plastic container using an old sieve or colander.
3 Return the water to the saucepan and add the vinegar (this acts as a simple mordant).
4 Gently wash the fleece in warm water using a little washing-up liquid; rinse, then add to the saucepan.
5 Slowly bring the water back to the boil, then turn down to a simmer. Do not agitate the wool or boil rapidly, otherwise it will **felt**.
6 Rinse thoroughly, then leave to dry.

industrial dyes and dyeing

Industrial dyeing generally involves the use of **synthetic** dyes which, unlike natural dyes, can produce strong, intense colours. The other main reasons for using synthetic dyes rather than natural ones are that:

- they are cheaper to produce
- they are easier to manufacture
- they produce a consistent colour every time
- a huge variety of colours can be made.

Synthetic dyes can now be produced so that they suit the properties of particular fibres and fabrics. Dyes are absorbed differently by different fibres, so it is important that a dye be selected with the fibre content in mind.

Affinity of dyes

The chemicals used to make dyes are unlike the chemicals found in fibres, so the two do not readily bond together – there is no **affinity** between them. To help create an affinity between the dye and the fibre, as well as to improve **colourfastness**, **mordants** are used in the industrial dyeing process.

Stages of dyeing

Dyeing can take place at several different stages of the production process, and this will depend on the fibres used and the items being made.

- THE FIBRE STAGE – Dyeing the fibres themselves produces an end-product with a uniform colour because the dye has penetrated every fibre. Artificial fibres are dyed while they are still liquid and before they have been spun. Natural fibres are dyed loose in dye baths. A knitted jumper with a 'heather' effect is a good example of fibre dyeing, because the fibres are dyed different colours and then mixed together before the yarn is spun, giving the wool a random look.

- THE YARN STAGE – This process is comparatively expensive because the yarn cannot be dyed in loose form the way fibres are, because it would become very tangled. Instead it is wound on to special containers. Although the dye is not distributed quite as evenly as it is in fibre dyeing, this is a good way to get clear stripe or check effects when different coloured yarns are woven or knitted.

- THE FABRIC STAGE – This is a cost-effective method of dyeing, because fabric can be stored undyed, and dyed only when it is required. Stockings and tights are a good example of this, as the manufacturers can wait until they know which colours are selling well before dyeing takes place. This is sometimes referred to as piece dyeing, and is usually used only for plain-colour items. However, a patterned effect can be achieved if the fabric is woven or knitted using two or more different fibres and only one type of dyestuff. The different fibres have a different affinity for the dye, and so some areas will remain undyed. This is known as cross dyeing.

Sometimes dyeing takes place only when a whole garment has been made up. This is unusual unless it has a very simple design, because areas such as seams may be affected by the dye in a different way from the rest of the garment.

8

Environmental issues

Dyeing on an industrial scale is currently an important environmental issue. There are two main problems with dyeing.

First, the process requires vast quantities of water; and second, it results in unsightly and often toxic dye being discharged into the environment. Dye is not readily **biodegradeable**, and so new developments are being encouraged to find a different process that uses less water and does not do as much damage to the environment.

Clothes and accessories can be dyed easily and cheaply using synthetic dyes. A huge range of colours is available, and they produce consistent colours each time.

Allergic reactions

Although there are thousands of synthetic dyes, only 49 are believed to cause an allergic reaction. According to research, people in Mediterranean countries are more prone to textile dye allergies than those in northern Europe. This is probably due to the higher temperatures and humidity of those countries, causing more sweating and therefore closer skin contact with the dyed textiles.

testing dyes

All coloured fabrics are expected to have a reasonable amount of **colourfastness**, although dyes are not necessarily fast with every type of fibre. Colourfastness can be divided into two areas:

- the change in the depth of the shade of colour
- the transfer of colour from a dyed fabric to another fabric (staining).

Why do dyed colours change?

Many things can affect fabric dyes and cause a change or staining of colour. These factors are referred to as 'agencies'. They can be introduced by the consumer in the process of washing or dry cleaning the item, or exposing it to light, perspiration or abrasion (rubbing). Or they can occur during the manufacturing process – for example, heat and moisture during pressing, atmospheric fumes in storage, and chemicals used in special finishing treatments.

Many **dyestuffs**, as well as fibres themselves, can be affected by the ultra-violet light in daylight which causes a chemical change in the composition of the dye. This change can create compounds which then speed up the process of deterioration in fibres – a process that is accelerated even further by washing the fabric. The change in colour brought about by light is usually referred to as 'fading', which means a loss of colour strength. If a fabric is likely to be exposed to light for long periods of

time – e.g. curtains, beachwear, holiday clothes – then the dye selected should obviously have maximum light fastness.

Dye fastness

Fibres vary in their ability to hold dye. This can be tested in a laboratory by evaluating the colour change that occurs after the fibres have been washed. A sample of dyed fabric is washed in a washing machine with a multi-fibre test strip attached to it. This test strip consists of a piece of fabric divided into sections containing different types of fibre. So, there might be a section of wool fibres, a section of polyester fibres, a section of cotton fibres, and so on.

The fabric is washed at the correct setting for its type and then examined to see whether its colour has changed. The multi-fibre strip is studied to see whether any of the dye has transferred on to the fibres. The amount of colour change, or dye fastness, cannot be based on personal judgement, so a system known

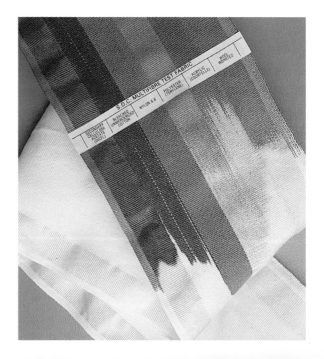

A multi-fibre test strip. This strip is used to assess the dye fastness of samples of dyed fabric. ▶

as 'grey scales' is used. The series of fibres are assessed using the grey scales measurement. It moves from no colour change seen, for which 'no change' is recorded, to total dye absorbtion, for which 'heavy staining' is recorded.

Dying results

If the test shows that the dye is not completely colourfast, a number of options are available. Firstly, the test could be repeated using a different machine wash setting, for example a cooler temperature. Or, if the dye did stain some of the other fibres the item could be labelled 'wash separately' or 'dry clean only'. Failing that, the fabric could be sent for re-dying or be totally rejected.

What makes a good dye?

To produce satisfactory results, a dye used for most textile fabrics needs to have the following properties:
* colourfastness
* light fastness
* perspiration fastness
* be insoluble in drycleaning fluids (dry clean only)
* be unaffected by salt water and chlorine (swimwear)

The fabric has to be tested properly to ensure that the correct dye has been chosen for the fibre(s) involved. There is a fast dye in most colours for every type of fibre.

An example of dyes that can produce a faded effect. This new colour technique causes the dye in a single length of yarn to change gradually. ▶

Desirable fading

A textile company in Huddersfield called Nuance Ltd are experimenting with dyes that have the effect of fading into one another. The dye in a single length of **yarn** changes while the yarn is being manufactured, producing perfect continuity rather than a series of breaks in colour. The company specialize in high-quality cashmere and cashmere/silk yarns, and have produced a range of knitwear using their new colour technique.

inspired ideas

New textile items appear on the market every day. Perhaps this is not so surprising, given that the term 'textiles' covers a huge range of products, from domestic to industrial. However, new ideas have to come from somewhere – and anyone involved in textile design, from GCSE students to professional designers, must be constantly on the lookout for innovations in textiles.

It is rare for someone to think of a unique idea without any prompting. When a need has been identified, textile designers are often given a **design brief**. This states the intended use of the product to be designed. Most **design ideas** are the solution to a problem, and it is not necessarily the person who has identified the problem who goes on to solve it. Ideas may also develop from discoveries made during experiments or research; this has certainly been the case with many new fibres and fabrics.

Specifications

Once a problem has been identified and a design brief written, a great deal of research and investigation is carried out to gather information about what is needed. Its precise nature must be studied to ensure the need is fulfilled. This may involve talking to consumers, looking at similar existing products, and questioning experts about the technicalities of the problem. Research and investigation can take many months, even years, depending on the complexity of the idea to be developed.

If the results of the research indicate that the problem can be solved, financially as well as practically, then a design specification is produced. This contains details of what the designer will require in order to develop ideas. It will include the function of the product, cost limitations and types of material, as well as considerations that are specific to the **consumer target group**. Armed with the design brief and design specification, the textile designer can start to generate ideas.

Inspiration for ideas

It would be impossible to list everything that can be used as a source of inspiration when designing. Ideas can develop from things as casual as glancing in a shop window or chatting to friends – so the most important thing is to be observant; you never know when your observations might come in useful!

However, ideas do sometimes need to be prompted, so designers often have to carry out research while looking for inspiration. Colour swatches, fabric samples, **yarns**, threads, accessories, even items of jewellery or food can all help get the creative process happening. Inspiration may come through studying nature, art or music, by reading books, newspapers or magazines. It is also essential to find out as much as possible about the consumer target group – what influences them and what they like.

Trends in society

Just as fashion can be influenced by trends in modern society, so can other areas of design. Natural fabrics

▲ To capture the mood of a new product, a range of items are collected together on a mood board.

and neutral tones are currently favoured, so textile designers are using these for carpets and other soft furnishings. When people in the public eye show a preference for a particular trend or image, this often becomes popular with the general public and designers need to be aware of this influence.

Mood boards

A **mood board** literally shows the 'mood' of a product. It might contain swatches of fabric, yarn, threads and so on, or photographs and pictures – anything collected during the research that can be used to influence the design. A mood board is likely to indicate a colour scheme and will also reflect the feelings of the consumer target group. Working drawings (sketches) are sometimes added to the board.

By showing the mood board to the consumer target group, it is possible to get feedback about the images so that the ideas can be developed further.

Once a designer has finalized a design or range of design ideas, these can be presented to the **client** along with the mood board. By showing the mood board with the final design, the client can see how the idea developed and what influenced its development.

Design by nature

A collection of bags called the Parasite range has been designed using 'biomemetics'. This is the study of nature's way of adapting to its surroundings. The bags have a hard outer covering, imitating the protective shell of turtles, and straps that relate to spiders' webs!

tie-dye

Tie-dye is a way of adding colour, and therefore pattern, to fabric. It is a **resist method** of dying, other examples of which include batik, adire, tritik, Japanese shibori, Malaysian plangi and silk painting using a gutta resist. The resist method simply means that something is resisting or stopping the dye from getting to some parts of the fabric. In the case of tie-dye knots, string, rubber bands, paper clips, and many other objects are used to resist the dye.

Tie and dye

Tie-dye is an old and very simple method of creating patterns. During the 1970s, tie-dyed clothes and bags were very popular and, like many aspects of seventies fashion, they reappeared in the 1990s. This also links with the nineties trend for natural methods and a natural look, because tie-dye is a traditional textiles hand craft, often produced with readily available resources, including natural dyes.

Tie-dye involves knotting or tying the fabric very tightly at regular or random points. The fabric is then dyed but the areas constricted by knots or string are unavailable to the dye. Once the fabric has been left in the dye for the appropriate length of time it is rinsed and dried. The result is an irregular combination of undyed and partially dyed shapes on a coloured background. Unlike printing, tie-dye does not produce precise patterns that can be repeated time and again, so tie-dye designs can be regarded as a truly unique decoration.

▲ Tie-dye was a popular way of decorating clothes in the 1970s and 1990s. It is an example of resist dyeing.

Creating colours

Two colours can be mixed together to produce a third colour (see page 5), and this is how different **colourways** are achieved in tie-dye. For example, if a sample of white fabric is tied randomly and dyed yellow it will result in white patterns on a background of yellow. Then, if that same fabric is tied in different places and dyed blue, the white areas will appear blue, the yellow areas will appear green and the areas tied for a second time may be yellow or white! If this sounds confusing, have a go and see the effect for yourself!

Creating effects

In addition to knotting or tying the fabric, different effects may be achieved in other ways. Perhaps the pattern most often associated with tie-dye is circles that radiate out at intervals from the centre of the fabric. This circling effect can be produced by lifting a square or circle of fabric from the centre with two fingers, creating a 'tube'. String or rubber bands are then tied around the fabric at intervals. Once dyed, circles of pattern appear where the fabric has been tied.

Other tie-dye effects include scrunching up the fabric by hand into a ball and tying it on the outside very tightly. Alternatively, the fabric can be folded into pleats which are then secured at intervals.

Extra effects

It is also possible to create different patterns by tying small stones or pebbles in the fabric or trying out other methods of resisting the dye. For example, the fabric can be stitched as long as the thread will not absorb the dye being used. Paper clips, bulldog clips, even staples, can be used when experimenting with unusual effects.

Hot and cold dye

A number of commercial dyes are now available for use with tie-dye or other crafts, or just to alter the colour of a textile item. Cold-water dyes are easy to use – you only need to add a dye fix and some salt. The amount of fabric that can be dyed with one packet or tin is written on the label. Using too little dye for the amount of fabric can result in an uneven colour. If you prepare too much dye you can store the excess in a screw-top plastic bottle and use it on another occasion. The bottle should be clearly labelled and kept well away from food.

Hot-water dyes work in a similar way to cold-water dyes, but as they work at a higher temperature they are not suitable for all fabrics or textile items. Machine dyes are useful when you want to dye a large quantity of fabric, because the dyeing takes place in the washing machine.

◀ *Tie-dye produces an endless variety of effects and is easy enough to be carried out at home.*

batik

Batik is another example of the **resist method** of dyeing. The word 'batik' comes from Indonesia and means 'wax writing'. Although batik as a craft is practised mainly in Java and Indonesia, it is also popular in south-east India, Europe and parts of Africa, especially Nigeria.

Hot wax

Whereas tie-dye uses knots or string to resist the dye, batik uses hot wax. The benefit of melted wax is that it is absorbed into the fabric, hardening as it cools, and so prevents the dye from penetrating the fibres. The wax can be removed relatively easily after the dyeing has taken place.

The batik technique is often used on silk fabrics because they are naturally absorbant, although cotton and linen are also used. Many **synthetic** fabrics have poor absorbancy, and don't hold hot wax or absorb cold-water dyes very well. Any new fabric being dyed should be washed first to remove possible finishes or dressings that it may have been treated with. Once immersed in the dye solution, the wax often cracks, giving batik its characteristic marbled effect.

Melting points

When wax is melted for batik its temperature should not rise above 137°C. Different types of wax have different melting points, but it is best to use a combination of 50% beeswax and 50% paraffin. Wax specifically designed for batik can be bought from craft shops and suppliers, and usually comes in particles, making it easy and quick to melt. It also means a small amount can be melted at a time, if necessary. In doing batik it is essential to control the temperature of the wax carefully and to follow safety precautions, as hot wax can cause serious burns.

Tools of the trade

For best results, batik should be done while the fabric is held taut in a frame. This stretched position helps the fibres absorb the wax and makes it easier to keep the fabric steady. It also keeps the fabric and wax off the work surface.

Traditionally the hot wax is applied to the fabric using a special tool called a *tjanting*. This handheld tool consists of a small metal bowl with a very thin spout. The hot wax is collected in the bowl and carefully applied to the fabric using the spout. This allows detailed and intricate designs to be created, and the metal bowl helps to keep the wax melted while working. Brushes may be used as an alternative to the *tjanting*, or when large areas need to be covered in wax. However, it is not as easy to apply wax with a brush because the wax cools and hardens more quickly.

Reverse batik is another alternative if a *tjanting* is not available. The framed fabric is covered in hot wax using a large brush. Once the wax has set, it can be scraped away with a sharp tool, following the pattern you want to create. When the dye is applied, it is accepted by the patterned areas of the fabric, which are free of wax.

A batik wall hanging that has been hand-crafted in Sri Lanka.

Cold dyes

Obviously only cold-water dyes can be used for batik, so the wax does not melt again. A dye fix is used to prevent the colour from running when the fabric is washed, or when the wax is removed if it is removed using water.

Different colour effects can be achieved by repeating the waxing and dyeing of a fabric several times. For example, part of a design could be applied in wax and the fabric dyed red. Then, more wax could be applied to protect areas of the design that are supposed to be red, and the fabric dyed blue. The resulting fabric would have patterns in red, blue and purple.

Removing wax

After the batik has been dyed and the fabric is completely dry, the wax has to be removed. It can be scraped off, but any that remains has to be removed using heat. This means either placing the fabric in boiling water, or else laying it between layers of absorbant paper and ironing over the top of it. The heat from the iron melts the wax, which is then absorbed by the paper.

printing

There are various methods of applying colour to fabric that come under the heading 'printing'. Those that can be carried out at home or school are considered here.

Block printing

Block printing is one of the earliest forms of printing and, if done carefully, it can produce effective designs. Beginning with a block of wood, cut out a pattern on its surface to create a raised design. This must be done accurately as any marks in the raised part of the wood will be transferred to the fabric. Next, cover the design in paint, either by brushing it with paint or by dipping it into paint, so it is evenly coated, and then press the block down on to the fabric. Finally, lift the block off the fabric slowly and evenly. If another colour is required the first application of paint must be completely dry before the next one is added, and each colour uses a new block.

Screen printing

Unlike block printing, screen printing requires some specialist equipment. It is necessary to have a fine mesh screen and a squeegee which is used to spread the paint. Screen printing is time-consuming and, as a different screen is needed for every colour used, it can be expensive to do at home.

This method is useful for simple designs with specific areas of colour because the design is built up, one colour at a time. First, the design needs to be created in stencil form; so, for example, there might be one stencil for a flower stem and leaf (green), and one for the flower's petals (pink). The stencils are cut out of a thin sheet of card or plastic film which the dye cannot penetrate. The stem and leaf stencil is then placed inside the screen,

▼ *Students screen printing large areas of fabric.*

which is laid on top of the fabric. Green paint (which holds the dye) is put at the top edge of the screen, and the squeegee is used to spread the paint evenly across the stencil. In the process the paint pushes through the gaps in the stencil. Once this is dry a different screen, containing pink paint and the flower stencil, is needed to complete the picture.

Stencil printing

It is thought that screen printing developed from the Japanese technique of stencilling. To stencil, cut the desired shape to be printed (usually a small shape that will be repeated) out of paper or card. Then apply the stencil paint with a brush or sponge, to colour those parts of the fabric that are exposed by the stencil. Once again this technique must be carried out with care, to avoid smudging the printed shape. Keep the fabric as taut as possible and hold the stencils firmly in place. When the paint is dry the stencils should be lifted slowly from the fabric.

Transfer printing

This method of printing literally transfers a design from one medium to another. Commercially produced transfers are available for use on fabric, or one can use transfer inks/pens/crayons to produce a design, which is then transferred to the fabric. Transfers are created on special paper using **disperse dyes**.

Place the transfer, design-side down, on to the fabric and apply heat by ironing the back of the paper. This causes the dye to change from a solid to a gas, and soak into the fabric, where it returns to solid form. The dye is also made **colourfast** during this process. The only difficulty that can arise is remembering to create the design back to front!

And finally...

Not strictly printing, but probably the simplest method of applying colour to a fabric at home, is to paint directly on to the fabric. This can be done using fabric paints, pens or crayons. You apply fabric paints with a brush, just as you would paint a picture. However, as fabric is involved it is important to practise the design beforehand to avoid making mistakes. The paint can also be applied using a sponge to create a textured effect, or the paints can be used when stencilling.

▼ *Fabric pens can be used to add detail to designs, in conjunction with other techniques such as embroidery or quilting. Fabric crayons provide thicker lines and are useful for filling in larger spaces.*

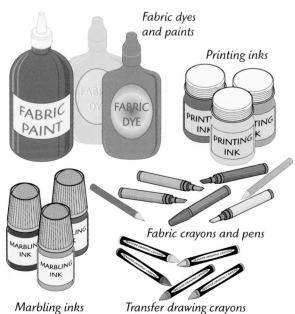

Fabric dyes and paints

Printing inks

FABRIC PAINT

FABRIC DYE

PRINTING INK

PRINTING INK

Fabric crayons and pens

MARBLING INK

MARBLING INK

Marbling inks

Transfer drawing crayons

textile project – ethnic cover-up

The following project involves making a computer cover, although you could easily adapt it for a television or other item of equipment in the bedroom or home – even making it into a cushion cover. You decorate the cover fabric first using tie-dye, to give it an ethnic look. The measurements given here will make a cover to fit most types of computer, but check the size before you start.

Decide on the colour scheme you wish to have and the effect you wish to create. It may be worth reading through the section on tie-dye again to remind yourself what is involved.

What you will need

- Calico – a plain weave cotton fabric, which is available in bleached or unbleached versions and in different weights; it is useful for dyeing. Alternatively, a plain cotton fabric is suitable. You will need 112cm of fabric (make sure the width is at least 115cm).
- Sewing thread, pins, needles, and a sewing machine.
- Cold-water dye, dye fix and salt, old washing-up bowls or buckets, rubber gloves, apron, old spoon, string, elastic bands, paper clips etc., an iron and ironing board.

Before decorating your fabric, cut out the three shapes that make up the computer cover. This is not essential, but it is often easier to work with smaller pieces of fabric when decorating with dyes.

Lay the fabric out on a flat surface. Following the line of the **grain** and using pins, mark out three oblongs. One should be 112cm x 45cm and the others 42cm x 40cm. Carefully and accurately cut out the three shapes.

If the fabric feels stiff or has a finish on it, rinse it in cold water and leave to dry before you start to decorate it.

Decoration

Prepare the cold-water dye and fix according to the instructions on the packet. Tie the fabric in a random fashion using the string, elastic bands, paper clips etc. For the tie-dye to be effective, the ties must be very tight, so the dye cannot penetrate through.

Place the fabric in the prepared cold-water dye and leave for the recommended amount of time. Make sure the fabric is fully submerged, otherwise it will look patchy. Remove the fabric, squeeze out any excess dye, then rinse in cold water until the water runs clear. When the fabric is completely dry, untie it, iron out the wrinkles and admire the effect!

Making it

Note: you should allow 2.5cm seams throughout.

1 Hem the two side pieces: for both pieces, press 2.5cm of fabric on to the wrong side along *one* 42cm edge; turn under again, press, pin and machine sew both hems.

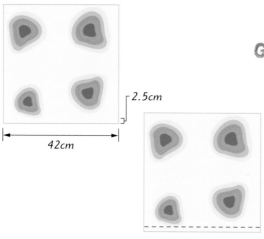

4 Tack and sew together: secure the side pieces with **tacking stitches** (large stitches that are later removed), then machine stitch the sides. Take care at the corners.

5 Finishing touches: remove the tacking stitches. Trim 5mm of fabric away from the seam. Iron the cover, pressing the seams open. Turn the cover the right way round.

2 Hem the main piece of fabric: at both of the narrow ends, press 2.5cm of fabric on to the wrong side, turn under again, press, pin and machine sew.

3 Attach the sides to the main body of the cover: with *wrong* sides of fabric facing outwards, pin one side to the long piece of fabric, starting at the hems and gradually working all the way around to the other side. Repeat with the other side.

Wrong side of fabric

Once you have mastered the computer cover, you could go on to make a matching keyboard cover!

Alternatively...

You could use batik, fabric painting, printing, even patchwork and quilting for this computer cover. Another very simple but effective way to create a bit of a splash on fabric is to use a spray diffuser. You place one end of the diffuser in a pot of slightly watered-down fabric paint. Then, as you blow air through the mouthpiece, the paint cascades out the other side – a useful tool to combine with stencils, producing a simple but effective design.

industrial printing

Industrial fabric printing is based on traditional hand methods, but is obviously a much faster process. Vast quantities of fabric have to be produced for the mass production of textile items. The print on the fabric must also be precise in order to meet high standards of colour and pattern consistency. The three main types of industrial printing are screen printing, block and roller printing, and transfer printing.

Screen printing

Screen printing accounts for about 78% of all fabric printing in the UK. It uses the same principles as small-scale screen printing but is carried out using large machinery. Rotary screen printing is commonly used in industry because it allows the production to be continuous, making it more cost-effective. The screens are cylindrical and their circumference determines the size of the design repeat. A different colour, in the form of printing paste, is pumped into each cylinder and continuously squeezed through the fine mesh screen on to the fabric moving beneath. More than 300 metres of fabric per minute can be printed using this method!

An alternative method is flat-bed screen printing, whereby the fabric is held flat on a surface using a special adhesive. The screen is held above the fabric by a conveyor which automatically moves along the fabric, one screen width at a time. As the screen is lowered on to the fabric, printing paste is applied to the screen and a squeegee or roller forces it through the mesh. The screen is then lifted and moved on to the next section of fabric.

▼ Industrial screen printing.

Block and roller

The traditional method of printing with blocks is modified in industry with the use of rollers. The rollers have a copper surface from which a design is cut. A separate roller is used for each colour. The printing paste is fed into the rollers and then pressed on to the fabric passing below. A design can be built up by having a series of rollers containing different colours, arranged around a drum. The design is complete when the fabric has passed under all the rollers on the drum. Roller printing does not produce detailed designs as well as other methods, and it is also relatively slow and expensive.

Transfer printing

Transfer printing is most successful on **synthetic** fabrics such as polyester. It requires the application of heat and the use of special dyes. Initially the design is printed on to paper using **disperse dyes**. Then the paper is placed on the fabric, printed-side down. The fabric is subjected to a high temperature by means of a heated **calender** which causes the dye to change into a gas. Once in the form of a gas, the pigments of dye are not attracted to the paper but attach themselves instead to the fibres of the fabric, where they return to their solid state.

Transfer printing is a relatively cheap process. It is also more environmentally friendly than other printing methods because it does not require water or produce any pollutants. It also produces a fabric that is **colourfast** straight away. However, on the negative side, it is more difficult to know precisely what shade of colour will be produced by transfer printing. As high temperatures are involved, it can be used only with a limited range of fabrics.

Some other ways to print on textiles

- Resist printing – using the **resist** principle of tie-dye or batik, this method involves applying a resist to the fabric to prevent the dye penetrating certain areas. The resist is actually printed on, so once the fabric has been dyed and the resist removed, the printed area is free from colour.
- Discharge printing – this is a bit like printing in reverse! The fabric is dyed first and then overprinted with a paste containing a chemical that will destroy (or discharge) the dye. The areas that have been overprinted show a different colour from the background of the fabric.
- Flock printing – this method is frequently used on furnishings and wallpapers. It involves applying an adhesive to the fabric and then adding cut fibre snippets to provide a textured effect.

applying patterns

One way to apply colour and pattern to a fabric is by attaching other fabrics to its surface. This is the basis for the technique known as appliqué. Appliqué is the application of one piece of fabric to another by means of stitching. It is a textile craft with a long history, and it is still popular in many countries including India, Russia, Pakistan, Central and South America. Appliqué is functional as well as decorative, because by adding layers of fabric a garment or textile item can be made more durable (hard-wearing). It is also useful for patching up fabric that has become worn or ripped.

Appliqué has **aesthetic** as well as functional qualities. For example, quilts, wall hangings, pictures and cushions can all be given the unique '**collage** look' that is achieved through appliqué. Pictures can be created by cutting out shapes in fabric and sewing them on to a background material, or **abstract** designs can be created from scraps of fabric and coloured threads.

Planning appliqué

First of all, it is necessary to have a design for the appliqué (unless the design is to be created as you work, in which case it is good to think about a theme or a colour scheme). The design may be something that can be copied from a book, magazine or painting, or it could be designed specifically for the appliqué. It is important to remember that each area of the design has to be cut out in fabric and stitched on to a background, so it should not be too small or intricate.

When planning a piece of appliqué work it is important to consider the types of fabrics being used. For example, they might be all cotton, or all of natural origin. If they need to be easy-care fabrics, **synthetic** fibres might be the best choice. On the other hand, designs often need lots of different textures and colours which can be produced only by choosing a wide variety of fabric types. Whichever fabrics are chosen, they should be cut so their **weft** and **warp** threads run in the same direction as those of the background material. The background material should also be sturdy enough to hold layers of fabric.

Another important consideration in choosing fabrics is whether or not they fray. As appliqué involves stitching around the edges, the edges of a fabric that frays badly need to be turned under before stitching. A fabric like felt does not fray so it can be a useful choice.

Hand appliqué

All appliqué was traditionally done by hand. Although this is a time-consuming method, it is still very popular, particularly with smaller textile items such as **motifs** for sweatshirts.

Before cutting out the shapes to be used, apply a fine, iron-on **interfacing** to provide added strength. Then, starting with the background shapes first, and working up to those on the surface, pin or tack the design in place. When sewing the fabrics it is best to use a herringbone stitch if they fray, or for turned or

▲ *An appliqué design. The technique of appliqué is an excellent way to embellish textile items. Beads, sequins and even tiny mirrors can be part of the design.*

unturned edges use slip stitch or hem stitches. Threads of contrasting colours can add to the design.

Machine appliqué

Fraying is not such an issue with machine-stitching because satin stitch completely covers the edges of the fabric. Alternatively use a very close zig-zag stitch, or a stretch stitch if the fabric is stretchy. It is important that the shapes be tacked in position before stitching, or they are likely to move, even if held by pins. Also it is worth practising stitching around corners and curves before embarking on an appliqué design.

Special effects

Like so many textile techniques, appliqué can be combined with other methods of decorating fabrics. For example, padded appliqué can add texture and a raised effect to an otherwise flat design. By cutting out some wadding, slightly smaller than the shape that is to be padded, and then placing it under the fabric shape and stitching as before, a particular area can be emphasized. This can be further enhanced with beads, sequins, buttons or even tassels.

patchwork patterns

Patchwork is the traditional craft of joining pieces of fabric to form a larger unit of patterned fabric. In North America the craft dates back to the settlers of the early seventeenth century. They did not have much money, and used the technique as a way of creating a comfortable home using every last scrap of fabric.

Patchwork shapes

The shapes in a patchwork are usually straight-sided – squares, diamonds, triangles, pentagons, hexagons etc. This is because they have to fit together without any gaps. The main characteristic of patchwork is the interesting effect produced by the fabric pieces after they have been joined.

A one-shape patchwork is the easiest type to make because all the pieces are the same size and shape. The pieces may all be the same colour, but when several colours are used together, it creates a more interesting design.

All other patchwork is known as block-unit patchwork. This is because the fabric pieces are first joined into a block that is regarded as the basic shape, and that shape is then repeated throughout the patchwork. Even random patchwork designs can be of a block type, because patterns that use the same range of fabrics are created in blocks, e.g. squares, and then all the blocks (squares) are joined together.

Preparing for patchwork

Before beginning, consider the end-use of the fabric. If it is to be made into something that will need to be washed, all the fabrics used must be suitable for washing and ironing at the same temperature, or all must be dry cleaned. Unlike appliqué, it is best to use fabrics of a similar weight and construction so they can be joined easily, and so that one fabric does not have a dominating effect in the finished patchwork. Medium-weight, evenly woven fabrics work best, although this very much depends on the desired effect and end-use of the patchwork.

Designs can be prepared using graph paper and coloured pens. It is then possible to experiment with shapes and colour schemes as well as calculating the amount of fabric needed. Each shape within the patchwork requires a paper or thin-card template. These templates are used for cutting out the fabric, and they should be the exact size of the desired patchwork shape. Cut the fabric shape slightly larger than the template, so the edges can be folded over and **tacked** in place (see the diagram). Ready-made templates and fabric patches can be purchased from craft shops. Once the patches have been joined, either by hand or machine, remove all the templates.

Patchwork by hand

Patchwork is time-consuming when it is done by hand, as every piece of fabric must be carefully joined to the next so the stitches are invisible on the right side. The type of over-sewing needed is illustrated in the diagram.

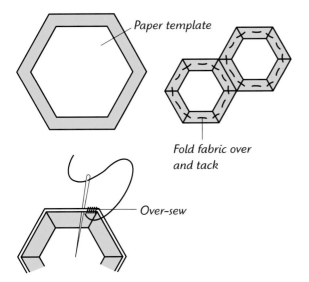

Over-sewing patchwork.

Paper template

Fold fabric over and tack

Over-sew

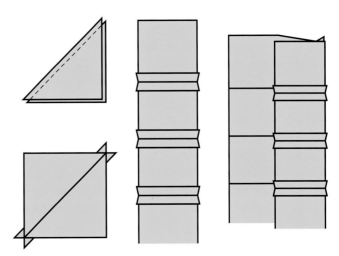

Machine patchwork using squares.

Machine patchwork

Patchwork can be produced a lot more quickly if it is done by machine, and with the current interest in recycling, patchwork has once again become popular. Today patchwork is evident in fashion items such as jeans and jackets. The simplest type of machine patchwork to produce is based on squares. Once a series of squares has been joined to form strips, these can be sewn together in one go, along the edge (see the diagram). However, it doesn't take much alteration of shape, size, colour and combination of fabric to produce an endless number of designs.

3D patchwork

Patchwork is an excellent medium for producing three-dimensional (3D) textile items. Consider the soft toy balls given to babies; they are often made from patches of felt fabric, usually in bright primary colours. The shapes are cut out of flat fabric, but when joined together they form a 3D ball, like segments in an orange.

One way of giving fabric a 3D effect ▶ is to combine colours and shapes carefully.

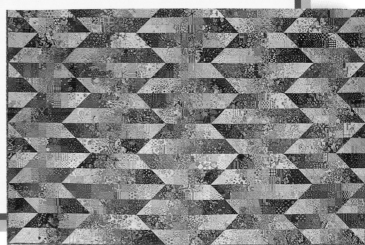

quilting

A quilted fabric is an example of a layered fabric; a layer of woven or knitted fabric on each side of a layer of **wadding**. The wadding is held in place with stitching, often in a decorative pattern. Quilted fabric is used where warmth is needed – for example, jackets, body warmers, table mats and bedding.

Insulating properties

Quilting a fabric provides insulation because air is trapped both within the wadding and between the layers of fabric. Wadding tends to be made from a washable polyester and is designed to trap air within its structure. The light texture of wadding means it is not very durable, so the outer layers of fabric prevent it from deteriorating. The stitching used in quilting must be kept to a minimum, otherwise areas of thin fabric are created and the insulating effect is lost.

Decorative effects

Quilting is more than just a functional fabric, because the stitching used to hold the layers of fabric in place can be applied decoratively. Also, as quilting involves padded areas of fabric, it can provide depth and texture to textile items. Quilting can be combined with other techniques such as patchwork, to improve the **aesthetic** value of the product.

Quilting techniques

Like all traditional textile crafts, quilting was carried out by hand; but the process can now be done easily and quickly using a sewing machine. Quilting does require careful preparation to ensure that the stitched design is accurate and that the layers of fabric do not move during construction. Frames are used in the manufacture of industrial quilts, or if large pieces of material are involved. The quilting design is marked on after the three layers of fabric have been assembled and set into the frame.

To quilt on a small scale, secure the layers of fabric by stitching a cross through the centre of the fabric (see the diagram). This also acts as a guide for the design. The design can then be marked on the outer layer of fabric using **tailor's chalk** and/or **tacking stitches**. The lines must be measured very accurately to avoid a distorted pattern. If the pattern requires straight lines and the outer fabric is fairly thin, you can place graph or squared paper behind it and use it as a guide (before sewing the three layers together).

▼ *Layers of fabric are secured by stitching a cross through the centre.*

Quilting stitches

The thread used for quilting can be a colour that contrasts with the fabric, but in this case it is even more crucial that the stitched lines are sewn straight, as a contrasting colour will make them more obvious. Most domestic sewing machines have a quilting 'foot' which helps to act

as a guide. This is an adjustable crossbar which runs along the previous line of stitching to ensure the next line is parallel to it. The foot also has upturned 'toes', so the thick wadding can pass freely under them.

It is possible to create a completely random quilted effect by stitching without a pattern, developing a unique design as you stitch.

Italian quilting

Italian quilting produces a fabric with a raised design and requires a padding **yarn** rather than wadding. A layer of fabric and **interfacing** are tacked together and the design is machine stitched on top using two parallel lines of stitching. The gap between the stitching provides a space for the padding yarn. With the reverse of the fabric uppermost, the padding yarn is threaded between the stitching, creating a raised design. The interfacing is cut at intervals so the needle and yarn can be pulled through and reinserted (see the diagram).

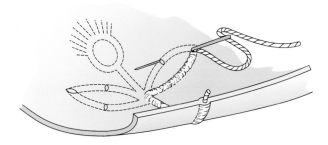

▲ *Italian quilting. The reverse of the fabric is cut at intervals so the needle and yarn can be pulled through and reinserted.*

Puff quilting

Padding yarn can also be used to achieve an effect known as puff quilting. This is where the edges of something like a pocket are given a padded look by machine stitching several parallel lines with spaces between them. The padding yarn is then threaded through the gaps and drawn through to the end. The reverse fabric does not need cutting with this technique, and the effect is to emphasize the edge of a garment or textile item.

Quilting by design

When designing a quilted fabric it is important to choose the fabrics and threads carefully, not just for their appearance but for their properties, too. For example, if you choose a stretch fabric the resulting quilted fabric will not stretch once it has been stitched.

sewing techniques

Apart from quilting, other methods of enhancing fabric by means of surface decoration include pintucks and piping.

Pintucks

Pintucks are folds of fabric held in place with stitches, and they range from a couple of tucks, for example at the waistband of trousers, to a whole series of tiny tucks. Pintucks can serve a purpose as well as being decorative, because they give shape and fullness to an area of fabric where it is required.

Functional pintucks are used at the waistband of skirts, trousers and shorts to allow for the fact that people usually narrow at the waist, so unless the waistband is elasticated, more fabric will be needed below the waistline. Pintucks are also used at the shoulder or yoke of women's dresses and tops to provide fullness for the bust.

Decorative tucks are used on many garments, particularly shirts. Very formal dinner shirts have rows of pintucks running down the front, each side of the buttons and sometimes around the neck instead of a collar. Pintucks are perhaps less obvious in household items, yet many sofas have a frill of tucks around the bottom edge. Duvets and cushions are often effectively decorated with pintucks which provide a surface interest without adding more in the way of colour.

Making pintucks

Pintucks are very easy to do, although when they are small and there are many

▲ *Tucks are often used at the front of trousers to provide fullness and shape.*

of them it is important to measure and sew accurately. Commercial patterns often indicate pintucks using lines, and these markings have to be transferred to the fabric. The fabric is then folded from one line to the other and secured, first by ironing, then by pinning and sewing. The tucks may be stitched across the top or stitched down their length.

When designing textile items with pintucks it is important to consider the direction of the tucks – for example, pintucks at the waistband are usually folded towards the centre. Extra fabric has to be allowed for tucks, and items containing a lot of pintucks are usually more expensive because of the added fabric and labour.

Piping

Piping is a technique that is likely to be associated with furnishings, as the edges of sofas, chairs, car seats and cushions are often piped. Piping is the addition of a cord covered in fabric along the edge of a textile item. The cord can vary in thickness, and the fabric may match or contrast with the main material. Piped products can be relatively expensive, as they require more fabric and more labour than unpiped versions. However, piping provides a neat finish and added visual interest.

On the bias

The fabric used to cover piping cord must be sufficiently flexible to encase the cord and to bend around corners where necessary. It should not be too bulky and, although it contrasts with the rest of the fabric, it should have similiar care instructions. In order for the fabric to be sufficiently flexible it must be cut on the bias. The bias of a fabric runs diagonally across the fabric's weave. If a strip of ordinary woven fabric is cut along the **weft** or **warp** it will not have any stretch, but if a strip of the same fabric is cut diagonally it will have a small amount of stretch. Special bias binding can be purchased and used to cover piping cord.

Piping method

In order to add piping to an item, you need sufficient lengths of biased fabric. If they have to be joined then this must be done beforehand (sewing diagonally with the bias). The fabric must be wide enough to cover the cord, with some excess to act as a seam. The cord should be long enough to pipe the entire area, if possible. First, wrap the cord in the fabric, right side showing, and secure with **tacking stitches**. Then place the prepared piping in the middle of two pieces of fabric, right sides facing. The piping must face inwards while the extra fabric acting as a seam touches the outer edge of the fabric. When all three layers are secure, they have to be machine stitched close to the piping. On turning the fabric round the right way, the piping will appear between the two layers of fabric.

▼ *Piping provides a neat finish and added visual interest.*

stitching gathers

Gathering is another example of a decorative technique that also serves a purpose. Like pintucks, gathers can give fullness to an area and make fabric curve – for example, around the top edge of a sleeve, so that the sleeve fits into the armhole. Gathering may be purely decorative and used to create a frill on a garment or item such as a bag. It can be seen on clothes and on soft furnishings.

Gathering principles

The principle of gathering is the same whether it is carried out by hand or by machine. Two rows of even stitching are applied to the fabric edge that needs to be gathered. Each row of stitching is secured at one end only, but at opposite ends to one another. This allows the fabric to be gathered from both edges, ensuring an even distribution of fabric. Once the gathered fabric has been attached in the appropriate place, the gathering stitches are removed.

Hand-stitching gathers is time-consuming and care has to be taken to ensure the stitches are the same size, otherwise the gathers will be uneven. Machined gather stitches are usually larger than normal machine stitches, so that the fabric is relatively easy to gather. However, the stitches can snap quite easily, so gathering should not be done too quickly!

Curtain gathering

Some curtains are gathered using a special curtain tape known as rufflette tape. Rufflette tape is sewn into the top of the curtain. It comes already prepared with threads for gathering as well as pockets for the curtain hooks, so the whole process of making gathered curtains is much quicker and easier.

As with all gathering, curtain fabric must be much wider than the actual size required. Different types of gathers use different amounts of fabric, and these are indicated on the rufflette tape. For example, pencil pleat curtains need three times the window width, while pinch pleat curtains need only twice the width. Two or three threads in the rufflette tape are specially attached so they will create a particular type of gather when they are pulled.

Smocking

Smocking is a decorative form of gathering. It has traditionally been sewn by hand on aprons, nightwear, and children's and babies clothes, but through the ages the smocked 'look' has come and gone with fashion trends. The recent 'peasant style' fashion uses smocking for blouses and dresses. Smocking is still popular for babywear and children's clothes because it gives children more freedom of movement, and space for bulky nappies. Young children have not yet developed a waistline, so clothes that are smocked at the chest provide room for their tummies. In addition, smocking can look very attractive and is often used in the design of Christening gowns.

How to smock

Today, smocking can be done quickly and easily by machine stitching and machine embroidery, so mass-produced clothes are smocked this way. To try out the technique you can smock a small sample of fabric, and this could even be included on a garment, perhaps as a pocket. First, gather the fabric, but instead of sewing just two rows of stitching to gather it, sew several rows (depending on the depth of smocking). The stitches should be close together so the fabric is not too bulky, and they should not be removed until the smocked fabric has been secured to another piece of fabric.

Once gathered, use embroidery stitches to decorate the surface of the gathers. You can sew stitches such as stem, feather and chain across the fabric, from fold to fold, to create a pattern.

◀ *Smocking and gathers are used to decorate and add shape to clothes.*

Honeycomb effect

The stitches illustrated below produce a 'honeycomb' effect on smocked fabric. Rather than stitching straight across in a row, stem stitches are worked up and down, creating gaps in the folds of fabric.

▼ *Producing the honeycomb effect of smocking.*

1

2

3

4

5

The final look

6

33

embroidery

Few forms of decoration have had such long-lasting appeal as embroidery. It is startling to realize that embroidery was carried out as long ago as 5000 BCE. Today, it is still a highly fashionable way of decorating clothes and accessories.

▲ *Some modern examples of embroidery.*

'Embroidery' can be defined as the application of coloured threads on to fabric in order to enhance the fabric's appearance. Different threads provide different textures, and patterns can range from tiny delicate designs to large areas filled in with stitching. Most types of fabric can be used for embroidery, as long as the weave is even and the fabric will not be distorted by the sewing. Threads are made from silk, cotton, wool, synthetic fibres, metallic fibres, even plastic. Intricate stitches look the best and are easier to create using fine threads.

Fancy stitches

There may appear to be an endless variety of embroidery stitches, but in fact many stitches are simply a variation of a particular type. For example, permutations of 'blanket' stitch include buttonhole stitch, closed buttonhole stitch and knotted blanket stitch.

Embroidery stitches are used in one of two ways: to create an outline or to fill in a shape or design. Of course, both types can be used together – for example, stem stitch may form an outline while satin stitch fills the space in the middle. Filling stitches can completely hide the fabric, or a lacy effect can be achieved by using open stitches such as feather stitch.

To do hand embroidery you usually need an embroidery frame, also known as a *tambour*. It consists of two wooden loops, one inside the other, with a fastening on the outside loop. The fabric

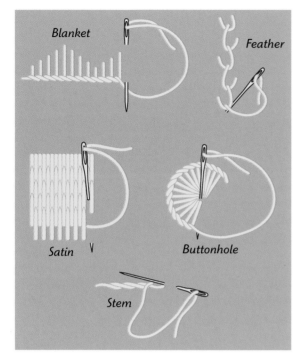

▼ *Some examples of embroidery stitches.*

Blanket

Feather

Satin

Buttonhole

Stem

is placed over the smaller loop, and then the larger loop is put over the top and fastened down tightly. This ensures the fabric remains taut and even while the stitches are sewn. Embroidery needles tend to be thicker than sewing needles, with longer, wider eyes.

Industrial embroidery

The textile industry uses special embroidery machines, often computer controlled, to produce embroidered items. Hand embroidery is a time-consuming process so it is not practical for large-scale production. Industrial one-off items (known as '**job production**') may be hand embroidered, but these are much more expensive because of the cost of labour and the fact that the item is unique.

By using software that has been programmed with designs, and machines that stitch the designs very quickly, embroidered items can be produced at prices affordable to most people.

Machine embroidery

Small-scale machine embroidery can be done at home or school using sewing machines that have a choice of embroidery stitches available. Some people own computerized sewing machines, which work in the same way as conventional sewing machines but have the ability to embroider stitches and designs that have been programmed into them. If attached to a scanner, a sketched design can be automatically stitched and even stored for repeated use. Some machines can be connected to computers so the screen is used for designing.

Thread painting

Embroidery may be thought of as a way of painting a picture on fabric using threads. The art of thread painting takes this idea further. You need an ordinary domestic sewing machine, as well as fabric fixed in a tambour, but in this instance the foot of the machine is removed. This enables you to move the fabric in any direction and so 'paint' an embroidered picture. Obviously, you can stop to use a new colour of thread and to change the type of stitch. This technique requires a lot of practice. You have to be in total control of the machine while you sew. However, it does enable you to produce items that are unique.

Thread painting is often combined with real painting. A picture is painted on to fabric, then areas are embroidered to provide texture, depth and added interest.

fancy clothes

To 'embellish' something means to enhance, decorate or improve it. For example, someone might embellish a story by exaggerating some of the detail to make it more exciting for the listener. Fabric can also be embellished to make it more exciting, by using techniques such as embroidery or the addition of details like buttons.

Appliqué and embroidery are techniques of fabric **embellishment** that we have seen already. Other ideas for embellishment include sequins, tassels, buttons, bows, knots, net, lace, zips, **motifs**, badges, beads, even jewellery. Embellishment adds interest and originality to products but it can also be used to jazz-up something that is old, faded or worn.

Clothes talk

Historically clothes have played a major part in revealing a person's status. Not just the fabric, but the style and detail of the embellishment have told us a great deal about a person's wealth and their position in society. For poor members of society, clothes could be little more than a form of protection, but the upper classes have used the appearance of their clothes to 'show off' their status.

Throughout the ages there have been some incredibly elaborate and highly decorated fashions which must have taken many months to make and were probably very uncomfortable to wear! This 'language' of clothing is less evident today, although uniforms are still used to

Queen Elizabeth I in 1592. Her dress is a shining example of the taste of the Elizabethan court: gold and pearl decorations, and the colour combination of coral red, black and white.

identify roles and occupations, and to many people the cut of a suit can say a lot about how much the wearer has paid for it. School uniforms not only identify the school a child belongs to, but they help to make all children feel equal, without the competition of wearing the trendiest garment.

An example of highly decorated clothes in relatively recent times is punk fashion. During the 1970s punks used safety pins and chains as a means of embellishment for their clothes (and often themselves!) Their clothes were usually black and enhanced with rips and tears. The **non-conformist** look was complete with hair formed into spikes, high on the head and dyed unexpected shades such as green or purple.

Dramatic costumes

Probably the only places to see elaborate historical clothes today are in period dramas and at the theatre. Period costumes for television have to be specially made and they must be as accurate as possible in every detail. It would be no good making a Georgian dress with a zip fastening! Just as the actors must study the period in order to act and behave in the correct manner, so costume designers must consider the fabrics, styles and methods of decoration and replicate (copy) them as closely as they can.

Theatrical clothes

People who are designing clothes for the theatre have additional considerations. The actors must be clearly recognizable

from a distance and their clothes must not clash with the scenery, or with each other. The choice of fabric may have to be richer in some cases or more fine and flowing in others. The colours may need to be bolder and brighter than normal in order to achieve the correct effect. Rather than having a few simple decorations, a garment may need many brightly sparkling glass beads or sequins that catch the theatre lights and add to the magical atmosphere.

extra embellishment

Weddings are important occasions in every culture, and where traditions are upheld they usually involve a great deal of 'dressing up'. People wear their best clothes, often using extra types of **embellishment** to make themselves look as special as possible. The type of decoration worn at weddings varies a great deal between different cultural-religious traditions. The focus below is on the Western (Christian) tradition of marriage.

Wedding bells

In traditional Western marriages, the clothes, hats, shoes, even gloves, are usually embellished in some way. Guests often wear flowers – women may wear a corsage, and men a 'buttonhole'. These add a splash of colour to an otherwise plain suit or outfit. Hats may also be adorned with flowers, fresh or artificial, and decorated with scarves, bows, beads and sequins. The shoes and gloves worn at such weddings are usually enhanced with embroidery and tiny glass beads.

Wedding dresses

In Western marriages (and many non-Western ones), the bride's dress is of central importance. The variety of wedding dresses available is endless, and original ones are still being designed. Brides often choose luxury fabrics such as silk, sateen, taffeta or damask, and styles range from the highly elaborate to simple dresses that would not look out of place at a less formal occasion. The traditional colour for a bride's dress is white, but popular colours include cream,

▼ *A beautiful embroidered bodice. Both the dress and shoes have been embellished for a special occasion.*

ivory, beige and pale gold. All of these tones can be enhanced with pearl beads, either stitched on to the bodice, attached to the veil or added to cuffs, necklines, waists and hems. Embroidered bodices, where the embroidery thread is the same colour as the fabric, are also popular.

Dress fastenings can provide an embellishment in themselves. Laces are used to tie the dress either at the front or the back, tiny pearl buttons with fabric loops to fasten them, or a large sash that ties into a bow at the back.

Male attire

The use of pintucks on dinner shirts has already been mentioned, and these are often seen at traditional Western weddings and other formal occasions. The choice of suits for men is very wide nowadays, so not everyone chooses to wear the extremely formal 'top hat and tails'. Waistcoats provide an excellent opportunity for embellishment, or they can be used to 'lift' the whole look by being made out of brightly coloured fabric. Sometimes the front of the groom's waistcoat is made of fabric that matches the outfit of the bride's attendants, such as her bridesmaid or pageboy.

Trendy embellishment

Weddings are not the only occasions when embellishment is obvious. Parties, theatre trips, clubs, restaurant meals, ceremonies – all provide an excuse to get dressed up. The clothes someone chooses to wear when socializing and relaxing can say a lot about the type of person they are, and perhaps the type of fashion they like to follow. Here are a few examples of different looks and how they use embellishment.

- The biker
  Never really out of fashion – leather jackets; trousers and boots, studded with metal; plenty of chunky zips. Leather belts and arm cuffs displaying the skull and cross-bones often complete the look.
- Eastern
  Gold bangles and beauty spots are a must. Fabric is either embroidered with gold or metal threads, or golden coloured designs are printed on afterwards. Sequins are an essential embellishment.
- Country and Western
  This one has a clear American feel, with lots of bright colours and embroidered jackets. Hats are important, as well as tassels.
- Casual
  Even those who prefer to feel comfortable and look casual whatever the occasion may be able to boast an embellishment. The most casual of clothes, the t-shirt, can be adorned with splashes of appliquéed colour or even a false pocket that is purely decorative.
- Sporty
  Sport and fashion have become intertwined in recent years. Although most sportswear would not be practical with any embellishment – apart from the brand logo that is often embroidered on – for some it is essential. Gymnastics, ballet and ballroom dancing, for example, all require a degree of adornment.

sparkling decoration

Fashion is a big dictator, in terms of what people wear and how they wear it, but technology plays an ever increasing role too. The current trend is for clothes made from fabrics that fit where they touch and are comfortable and versatile; Lycra® is a good example of this. Another fashion trend is for sparkle and decoration.

Brody International – a case study

In order to combine the stretch of Lycra® fabrics with the sparkle of sequins, Brody International, Europe's only sequin manufacturer, have developed a sequin with stretch. High-**tenacity** Lycra® is attached to the sequins, making a sequin-covered garment more comfortable to wear. A new system known as 'slinging' makes it possible for two high-tenacity **yarns** to be knitted into a straight 'trim', and this provides a base for the sequins. Previous methods have used static cotton threads, which limits the end-use of sequins on stretch fabrics. Now, it is easier to knit braids, trims and finished garments, and this means sequins may well appear in areas of the textile market where they have previously been excluded – for example, in lingerie and swimwear.

Sequin quality

When it comes to **quality control**, the latest method of sequin manufacture has sorted that out, too. Obviously it is important that the amount of stretch is controlled and always remains constant, and this is achieved by using a purpose-built tension meter. The meter also prevents an unequal balance of the two yarns as they are knitted, which would otherwise result in the trim being twisted.

Embellishing the millennium

The trend for embellished textile items seems set to continue well into the new millennium. Not only did people choose highly decorated clothes to celebrate the millennium's New Year, but they want to carry on with this attractive fashion. Brody International are proof of the increased demand, because they had to put on extra shifts in their factories during the build-up to the millennium and their overseas markets had growth rates of over 200%!

Now it is possible to have a sequin trim that stretches with the fabric, making clothes more comfortable.

All items used to embellish fabric, not just sequins, must match the trends in fashion, so it is now possible to find buttons with transparent effects that give a 'not quite there' feel to the fastening. Poly-vinyl-chloride (PVC) has been produced with special tortoiseshell or shot silk effects, and it is also possible to have PVC net. Zips are now even more functional as well as decorative (when they can be seen, that is!), because they come in waterproof and invisible varieties. Lace is no longer just lacy; it can also be manufactured with a rib, making it more versatile in the production of clothing.

Embellished fabric

Of course, with all these advances in technology it is not surprising that some fabrics simply will not need to be embellished because they will be part of the **embellishment** themselves. Fabrics can be created with a laminated plastic film embossed with tiny lenses. If such a fabric were used to make curtains, for example, then as people moved around the room the colour of the curtains would change as the lenses **refracted** different areas of pattern in the fabric.

Another example of a modern fabric with 'in-built' embellishment is a 'burnt-out' material. In this process a chemical is added to the fabric before it is printed with a pattern, then it is baked at a high temperature. This causes the pattern to burn away, leaving a fabric with a lacy appearance.

A fabric with a ready-made, highly textured surface is achieved using acids. These are added to the fabric, which initially becomes elongated before being left with a 'puckered' look.

▲ This effect was created by screen printing chemicals in a grid pattern. The synthetic fabric used is shot polyamide organza, which blisters in the process.

Fashion phrases

Fashion forecasters often use rather weird and wonderful terminology to describe trends. Here are some phrases used to describe fashions of the future: 'cool and delicate', 'biological and vegetal' (meaning 'from vegetation'), 'elegant and witty' and 'full of enlightenment'.

household decorations

Home decoration became big business during the 1990s and the trend is set to continue. Do-it-yourself or DIY stores are in every retail park, and many shops that once only sold clothes, such as Laura Ashley and Next, have moved into interior decor. The interest in home improvement in Britain can also be judged by the popularity of television programmes such as 'Changing Rooms'.

Perhaps not everyone is brave enough to have their neighbours decorate an entire room for them, but most people are keen to have a go themselves. And this is not just an adult interest; many teenagers and students want to express their personality and individuality by decorating their bedroom to suit their taste.

Embellishing a room

Giving a room a 'make-over' does not necessarily mean re-decorating the whole room and buying entirely new accessories. Although a lick of paint can brighten things up, this can also be achieved much more quickly with a homemade rug, a stencilled wall or a wall hanging. Embellishing a room can be easy if you think of detail rather than the room as a whole. Door handles can transform a chest of drawers in the way new buttons can liven up an old jacket. Separate handles can be found in many DIY stores, department stores and craft shops. They can have novelty value or they can give a piece of furniture a more up-market feel.

Lighting is a very important element in any room. Light shades can dramatically effect the amount and type of light given out. A kitchen requires a bright, clear light whereas a bedroom may need a more subtle tone. After removing the covering of an old light shade (either the existing one or one picked up at a car boot sale or secondhand shop) the frame can be re-covered with a new fabric. Tassels and beads can be added to create a really unique effect. You should take care when dealing with anything electrical, and the fabric, tassels etc. must be well away from the bulb to avoid scorching.

'Throws' have become popular items for many households. They can be light or heavy, ranging from thin cotton through to heavy wool, and come highly textured, plain or full of colour. The idea of a throw is that a square of fabric can be thrown on top of a sofa, chair or bed, to give it a new image. If a throw and a couple of scatter cushions are used to cover a bed they can turn a bedroom into a dayroom in an instant!

Creating an effect

Whether designing a room or an item to go in a room, one has to consider the overall effect. Different colours can create different effects, such as 'cool' blue and 'warm' gold, but the effects of a particular fabric or shape of an item are less obvious. For example, a rather serious, business-like image is created by a sofa that has a strong, smooth, fitted cotton cover, whereas a sofa with loose fitting covers, pleated at the bottom edge, creates a cosy, more homely effect. Windows with blinds can look more formal than curtains, and they can also give the illusion of more space.

Designing interiors at any level requires planning, preferably after doing some research. As we have seen, inspiration for ideas can come from all sorts of places, and a **mood board** is extremely useful for gathering thoughts and ideas and looking at the overall effect. If you have chosen a particular colour scheme, then collect items to suit that colour.

Ergonomics

Ergonomics, which is the study of the relationship between people and their environment, is involved in the design of all products. Highly complex ergonomic research may be necessary. For example, it is no good designing a totally original and attractive dining chair if it is too low for the person sitting to reach the table comfortably, or if it makes their back ache after five minutes. By studying the size and height of people and objects, designers for the mass market can ensure that their products match the 'average' person, if not everyone. One-off items, on the other hand, can be totally 'tailor-made'.

Interior design. Interesting themes can come from all sorts of places, so it is a good idea to collect items for inspiration.

resources

Books

The following books are useful for students studying GCSE Design and Technology: Textiles Technology:

Design & Make It! Textiles Technology Alex McArthur, Carolyn Etchells, Tristram Shepard	Stanley Thornes 1997
Examining Textiles Technology Anne Barnett	Heinemann Educational 1997
Textiles and Technology (UK edition) Adapted by Margaret Beith	Cambridge University Press 1997
Textiles Technology Alison Bartle and Bernie O'Connor	Causeway Press 1997

The following books are useful for more detailed information on dyes:

The Motivate Series: Textiles Andrea Wynne	Macmillan Education 1997
Textiles Properties and Behaviour in Clothing Use Edward Miller	B T Batsford Ltd 1992

I.C.T.

www.brody.co.uk
Sequin and textile manufacturer – see page 40

www.craftscouncil.org.uk/exhib.htm
Provides details of forthcoming arts and crafts events throughout the country

www.textile-toolkit.org.uk
Includes news, competitions, details of events and a chat forum for students. There is also a CD-ROM available for use as a teaching aid for GCSE textiles

www.worldtextile.com
Publishes a variety of textile-related journals

Places to visit

Colour Museum
PO Box 244
Perkin House
Providence Street
Bradford
West Yorkshire BD1 2PW
(Tel no: 01274 390955)
*The museum consists of two galleries,
'The World of Colour' and 'Colour and
Textiles'. In the former you can learn
about colour and how it is perceived
(even by animals). In the latter you can
find out about dyeing and textile printing
from ancient Egypt to the present day.
You can even use computerized
technology to take charge of a dye-
making factory and decorate a room!*

The Design Museum
28 Shad Thames
London SE1 2YD
*Exhibits focus on design evolution in the
20th century.*

Victoria and Albert Museum
Cromwell Road
South Kensington
London, SW7 2RL
*Textile exhibitions and Crafts
Council shop*

Syon Park, West London
(Tel no: 020 8560 0881)
*Arts and crafts events and shows
throughout the year, an arts centre and
needlecraft centre as well as house and
gardens to visit*

Embroiderers' Guild
Apartment 41
Hampton Court Palace
East Molesey
Surrey KT8 9AU
(Tel no: 020 8943 1229)
*The collection is international and
includes embroidered and stitched textiles
dating from the 1600s to the present day.*

Contacts

The Crafts Council
44a Pentonville Road
London N1 9BY
(Tel no: 020 7278 7700)
*Provides up-to-date information about
art and crafts exhibitions and shows; also
produces a magazine called Crafts,
available on subscription*

glossary

abstract not looking like anything in particular

aesthetic relates to the beauty of something rather than other considerations, such as usefulness (function)

affinity where things have a close similarity

biodegradable able to be broken down (decomposed) by bacteria

calender a machine which smoothes paper or cloth by passing it between two rollers

client a person or company who has commissioned (requested the services of) a designer to solve a design problem

collage a picture made up of pieces of different material, including paper, cloth, photographs etc.

colourfast term used to describe a fabric from which dye will not wash out or rub off

colourways the same design shown in different colours

consumer target group the group of consumers being targeted for a product because they are the ones most likely to buy it; e.g. elderly, teenagers, sports women etc.

design brief a short statement about the intended use of the product to be designed

design ideas sketches to illustrate ideas which fulfill the design brief; they may be annotated (labelled) and coloured

disperse dyes dyes that are chemically attracted to fibres rather than water

dye a substance added to textiles in order to give colour; natural and synthetic dyes may be used

dyestuffs another name for dyes

embellishment special decorations or adornments added to clothing and accessories to make them more attractive or interesting

felt the matting (or felting) of hair fibres if they are washed at too high a temperature, or too vigorously

grain the direction in which the yarns travel, so all woven fabrics have two grains

hue another word for colour

innovations something totally new and original

interfacing fine material used to support certain areas of garments and textile items

job production production of unique items; they usually involve a lot of time and skill and are relatively expensive to buy; sometimes called 'one-off' production

mood board a board covered with pictures, sketches, swatches etc. that is used to create a mood or feeling about a product to be designed; often used when talking to the target consumer group. Also known as a theme board

mordant a chemical that can 'fix' the dye so it will not wash out or fade

motif a repeated image or theme in an artistic work

non-conformist someone who does not wish to follow the common trends in society

quality control a way of checking the quality of a product during or at the end of its production

refracted bend in a ray of light when it hits glass or water

resist method a method of dyeing (batik, for example) that uses something to prevent (resist) the dye reaching the fabric

synthetic produced chemically, not naturally e.g. polyester

tack hold together using temporary stitches

tacking stitches used to hold a fabric in place while it is being sewn; a cheap thread is used

tailor's chalk used to mark out fabric for cutting; often flat with a sharp edge for marking fine lines; easily removed with a brush

tenacity the strength of a fibre

wadding lightweight but bulky fabric, often made in polyester, used to pad or stuff textile items; has a loose structure, so can trap air when needed for heat insulation; soft enough for toys or padding areas of appliqué

warp the vertical threads in a woven fabric

weft the horizontal threads in a woven fabric

yarn single strand of fibres spun together

index